Crunch Time!

Series 1 - Words & Sounds

By Viola & Zaida Stefano

VeeZee Publications

Copyright © VeeZee Publications Pty. Ltd. 2024
First published in Australia in 2024
by VeeZee Publications Pty. Ltd.
veezeepublications.com

The right of Viola Stefano to be identified as the author of this work have been asserted by her in accordance with the **Copyright Amendment (Moral Rights) Act 2000.**

All rights reserved. Under the **Copyright Act 1968**, no part may be reproduced, copied, scanned, stored in a retrieval system, recorded, or shared, by any means or in any form, without prior written & signed authorization from the publisher.

ISBN: 978-1-923120-04-4

A catalogue record of this book is available from the **National Library of Australia.**

Author: Viola Stefano
Illustrations, cover & internal designs: Zaida Stefano

Illustrations copyright © Zaida Stefano 2024
Design copyright © Zaida Stefano 2024

Disclaimer: The content presented in this book is meant for educational purposes only. The author & publisher claim no accountability to any entity or person for any liability, damage, or loss caused or assumed to be caused directly or indirectly as a consequence of the application, use, or interpretation of the material in this book.

Contents

Introduction 1-2

Apple Core word list 3-5

Series 1 - Core word sounds 6-8

I Like - Book 1 sounds 9-12

I Like - Book 2 sounds 13-16

I Like - Book 3 sounds 17-20

I Like - Book 4 sounds 21-24

I Like - Book 5 sounds 25-28

Apple B.L.O.S.S.O.M.S.

Balanced
Literacy
Objectives to
Support
Students
Obtain
Mastery of
Sounds

Our Core word readers & Decodable texts offer opportunities	
for teachers to:	**for students to:**
• Complement & consolidate various phonics programs (process shown on pg.2) • Explicitly teach Core/high-frequency words & support students to apply their knowledge to an array of texts	• Apply their knowledge of phonemes to these contexts • Revise known phonemes • Learn new phonemes • Recognize that several letters/letter blends can represent the same sound

Series 1: I Like - Sounds

This book lists the words in our **Series 1** Core word readers and Decodable texts. The Decodable texts are in our '**Series 1 - Lesson Plans & Activities**' book. The lists are shaped by the 'sounds' in words. The light pink blossoms in the '**55 Apple Core words**' list indicate which Core words have been used across **Series 1 (S1)**. The white blossoms indicate the focus sounds attached to each of our Core word readers and Decodable texts. The dark pink blossoms highlight revision opportunities.

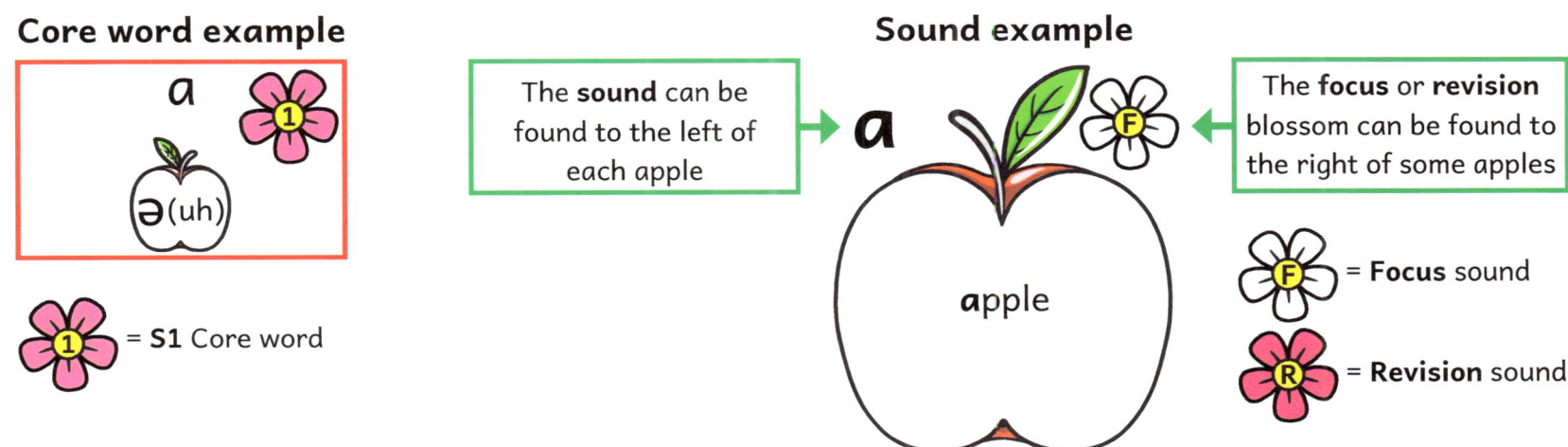

Teachers may include additional focus (**F**) sounds in their planning. These can be determined by sounds within the focus sounds. The focus sounds in **Book 1** include '**i**' and '**t**' (**i**n, **i**s, h**i**s, b**i**g, **i**t, h**i**t, k**i**t s**i**t/s, b**i**t, f**i**t, l**i**t, p**i**t, w**i**t & li**tt**le). Teachers may, for example, consider '**n**' as an additional focus sound as this is one of the sounds in the above list (i**n**). Refer to the additional focus sound list, in this instance, '**n**'. The words in the '**n**' list in **Book 1** are '**in**', '**on**' and '**can**'. These can be added to. Choose one or two of the words included and develop words around them, e.g., **in** (b**in**, d**in**, f**in**, p**in**, t**in**, w**in**) and **can** (b**an**, f**an**, m**an**, p**an**, r**an**, t**an**). Similarly, teachers may also add words to the focus word lists. Another focus sound in **Book 1** is '**e**' (T**e**d, Z**e**d, r**e**d, b**e**d, sh**e**d, sl**e**d, f**e**d). Words such as b**e**t, g**e**t, l**e**t, b**e**g, l**e**g, & p**e**g, or d**e**n, h**e**n, p**e**n, t**e**n, etc., could be included. Phonics programs can be used to guide word/sound choices.

 **Please note:** There may be regional sound variations in the pronunciation of some words. For example, the first '**e**' in 'envelope' may be pronounced as a short '**e**' (en) or as a short '**o**' (on). Further, specific '**schwa**' sounds (e.g., '**er**' as '**uh**') may or may not apply because of these accent variations. '**Schwa**' (**ə**) is a weak vowel sound.

VeeZee Publications - 55 Apple Core words & their focus sounds

I	want	can	stop
ie	w o n t	k a n	s t o p

like	more	he	go
l ie k	m or	h ee	g oe

here	what	do	the
h eer	w o t	d oo	th ə(uh)

out	where	we	it
ow t	w air	w ee	i t

not	they	when	that
n o t	th ae	w e n	th a t

VeeZee Publications – 55 Apple Core words & their focus sounds

help	off	you	yes
h e l p	o f	y oo	y e s
turn	who	this	no
t er n	h oo	th i s	n oe
done	make	a	to
d u n	m ae k	ə (uh)	t oo
come	in	some	which
k u m	i n	s u m	w i ch
open	get	good	same
oe p ə n	g e t	g oo d	s ae m

VeeZee Publications - 55 Apple Core words & their focus sounds

down	put	on	why
d · ow · n	p · oo · t	o · n	w · ie
under	**there**	**home**	**she**
u · n · d · er	th · air	h · oe · m	sh · ee
now	**them**	**is**	**look**
n · ow	th · e · m	i · z	l · oo · k
see	**and**	**up**	
s · ee	a · n · d	u · p	

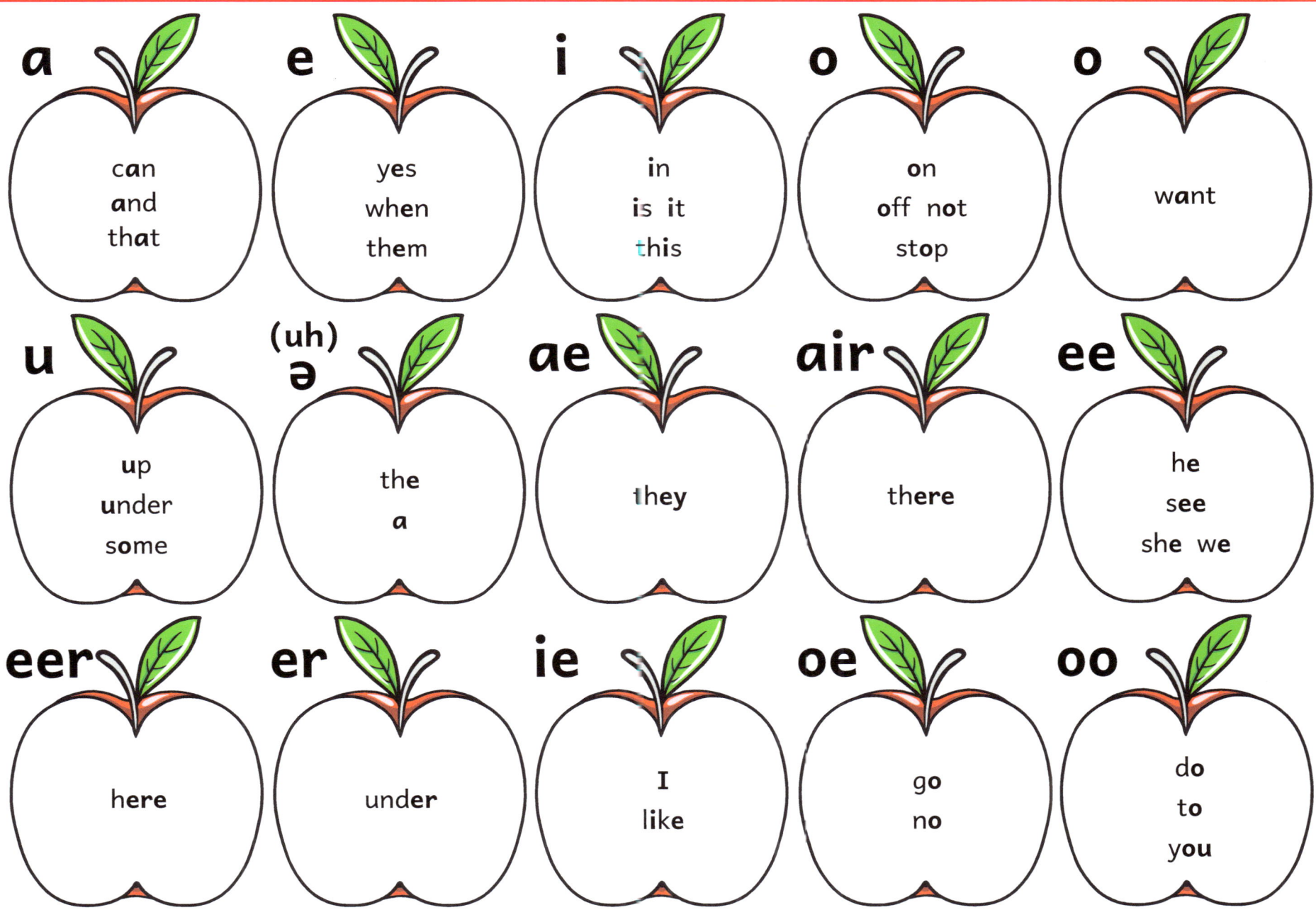

Series 1 – Core word sound groups

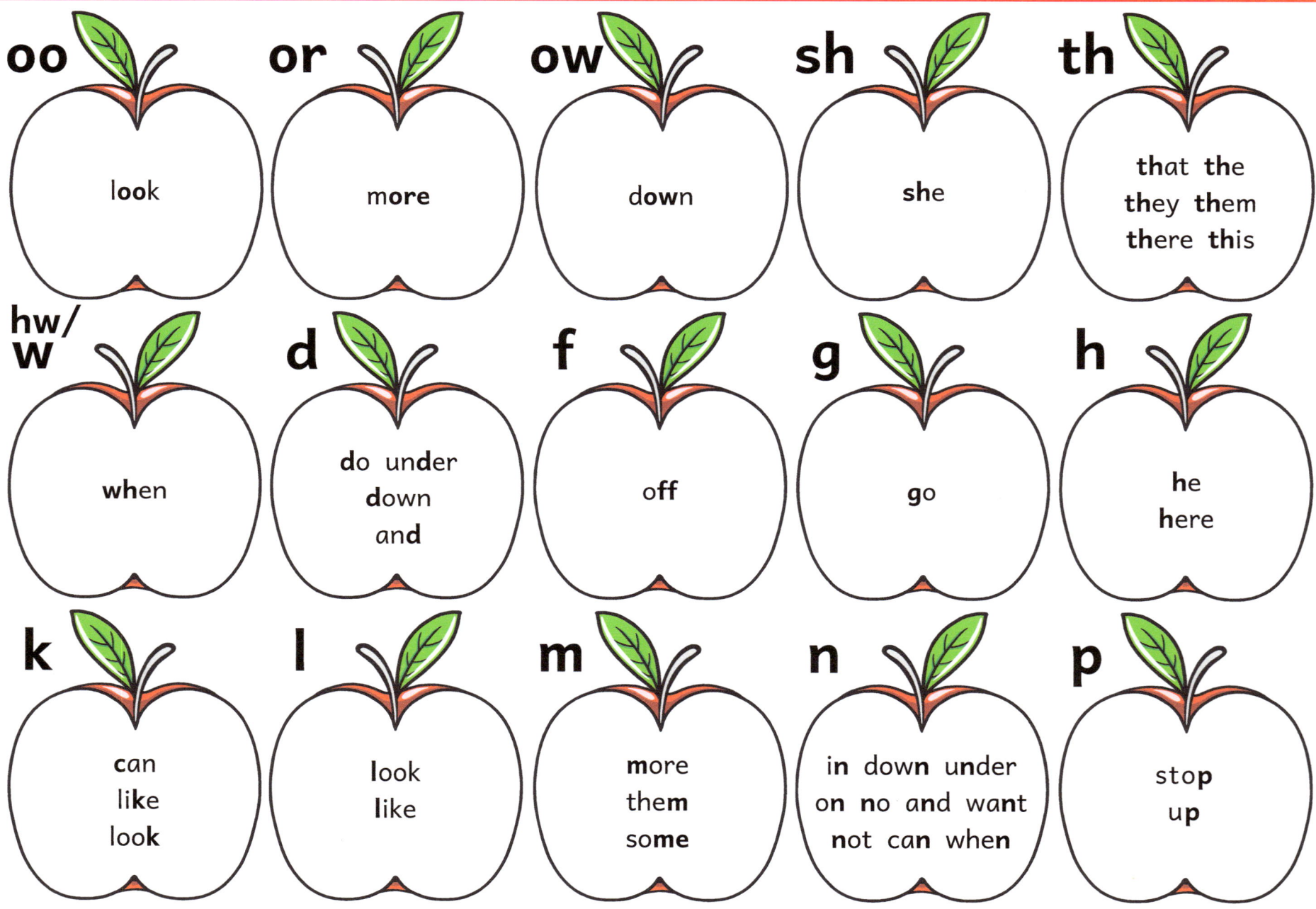

Series 1 – Core word sound groups

I Like - Book 1

Apple Core words in the Core word reading book	Other words in the Core word reading book
I, like, the, it, he, she	red, yellow, purple, orange, pink, blue, white, spider, beetle, ant, locust, bees, flowers, likes

Decodable text focus	Other words in the Decodable text
'ed' words: Ted, bed, red, shed, sled, Zed, fed	sits, on, his, little, he, can, see, a, big, it, is, in, the, cat, called, she, waiting, to, be, jumps, off, walks

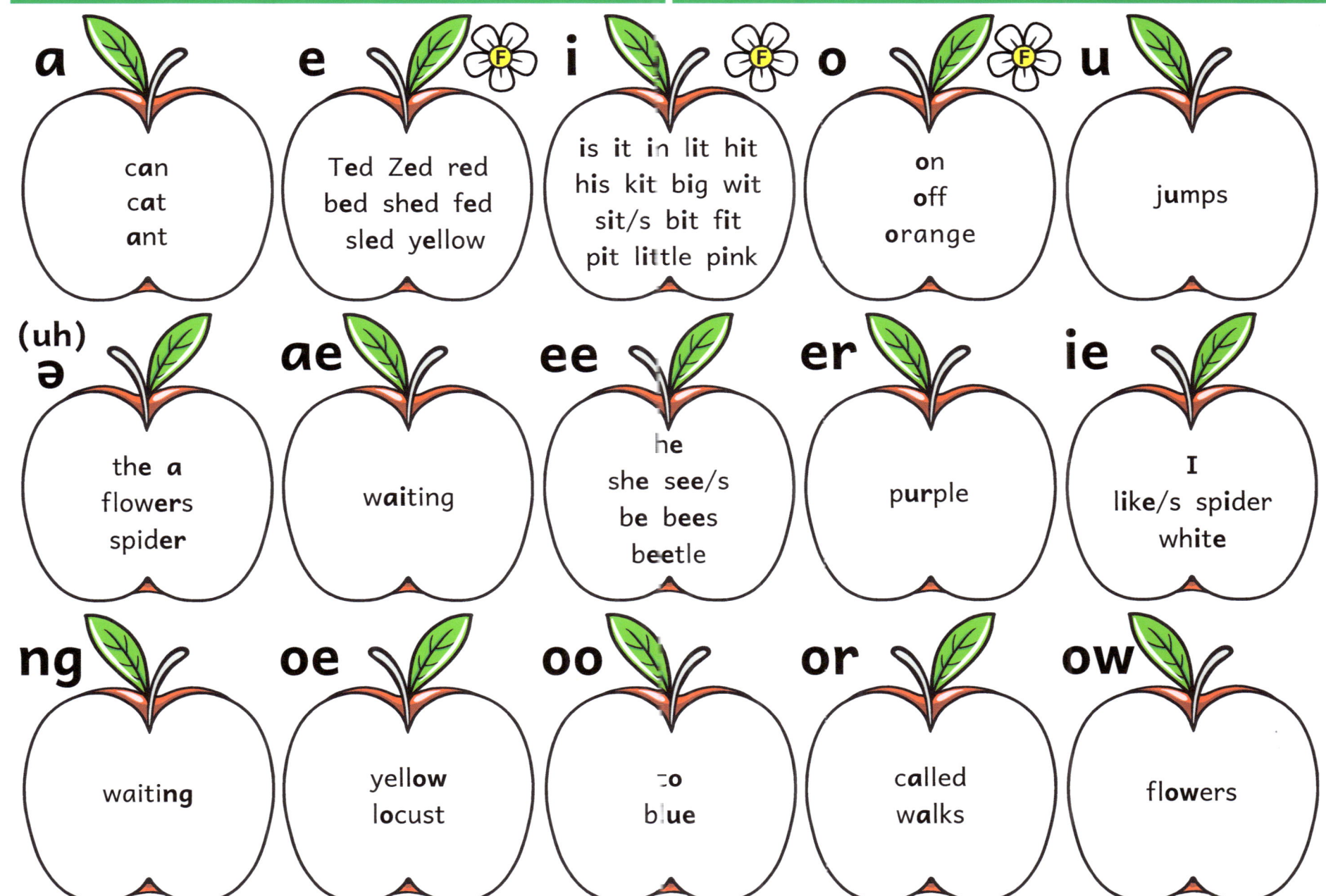

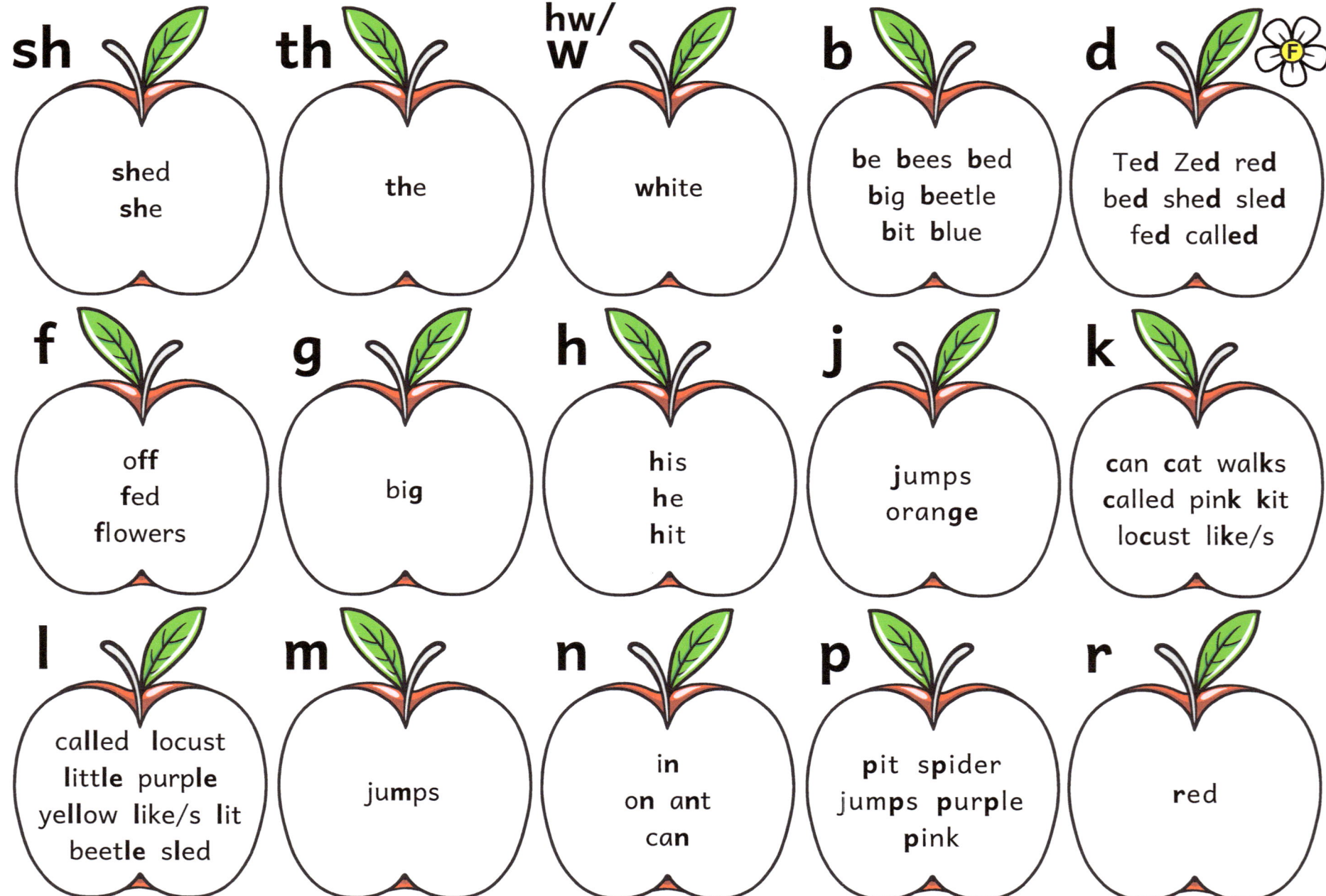

Series: 1 - I Like **Book: 1**

s — sit/s spider walks locust see sled jumps likes

t — it cat sit to kit bit fit hit locust lit

t — ant pit wit white Ted little beetle

w — walks with waiting wit

y — yellow

z — Zed bees is his sees flowers

I Like - Book 2

Apple Core words in the Core word reading book	Other words in the Core word reading book
I, like, the, it, he, she, more, they, we, you	mum, dad, bug, one, round, flower/s, long, short, tall, small, likes

Decodable text focus	Other words in the Decodable text
'all' words: small, tall, wall, hall, all, fall, ball, call	this, flower/s, is, and, that, one, you, like/s, the, I, she, close, to, he, they, are, blue, very, these, white, here, wind, some, of, them, roll, red, on, ground, like, little, stop, you, let, no, more, when

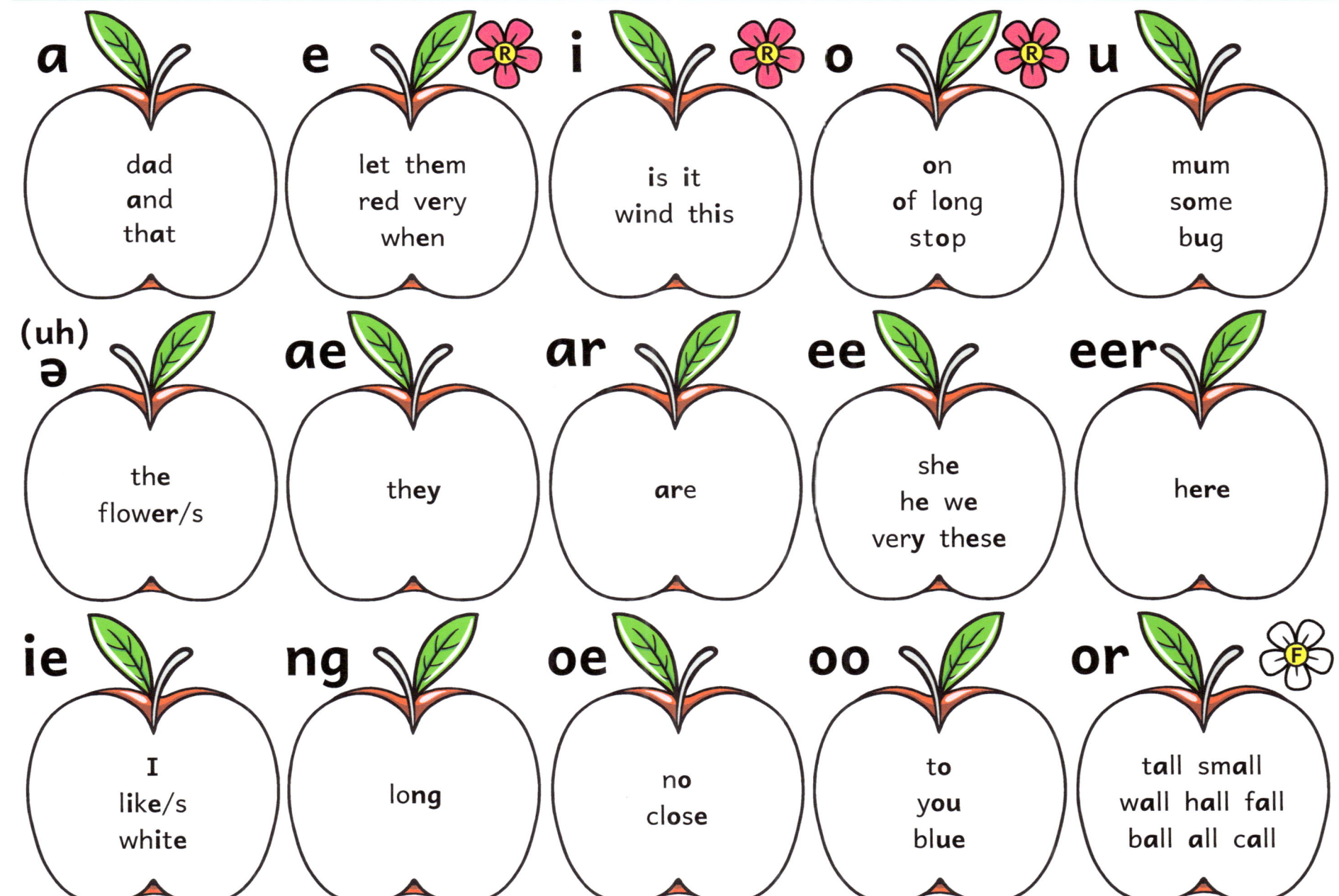

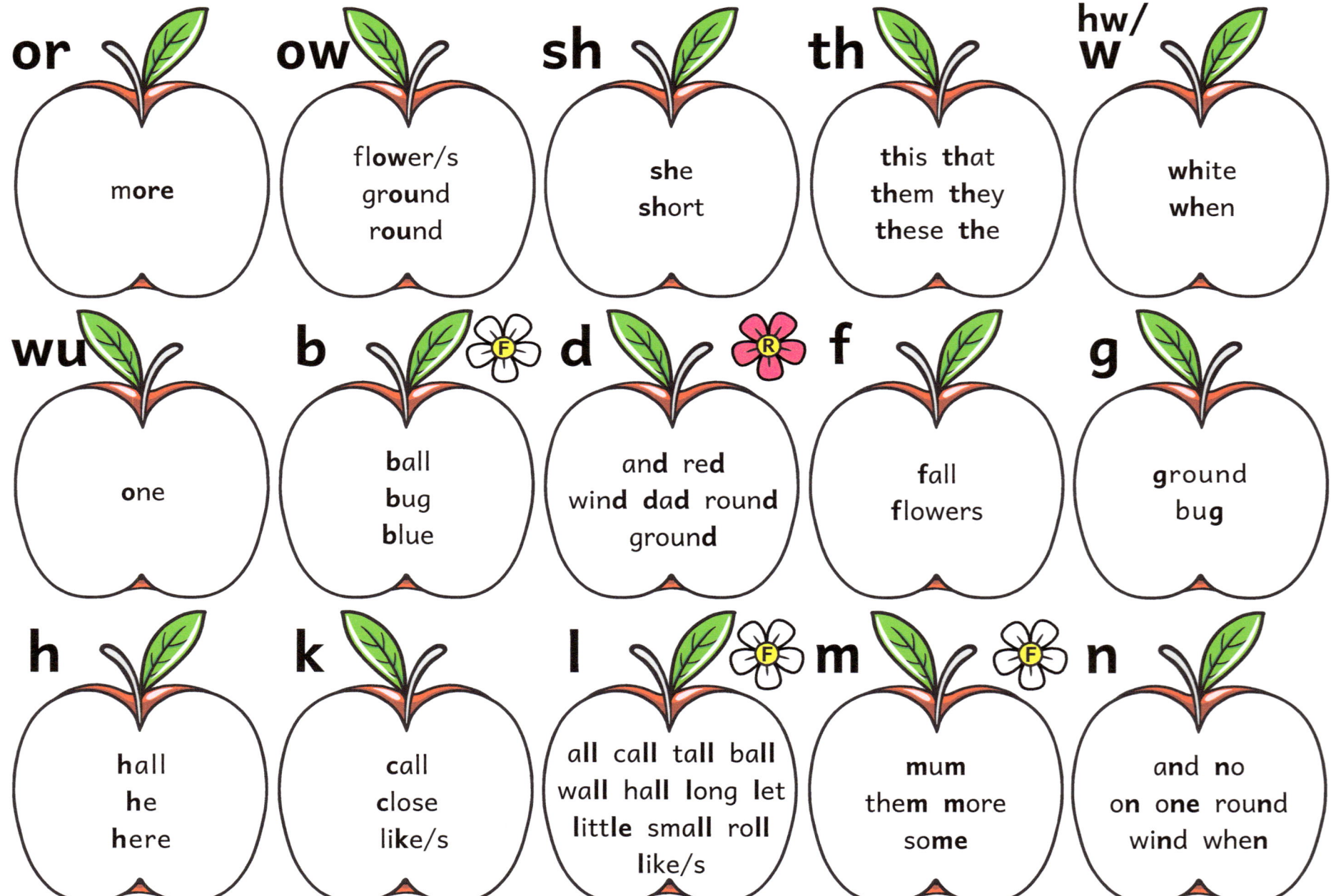

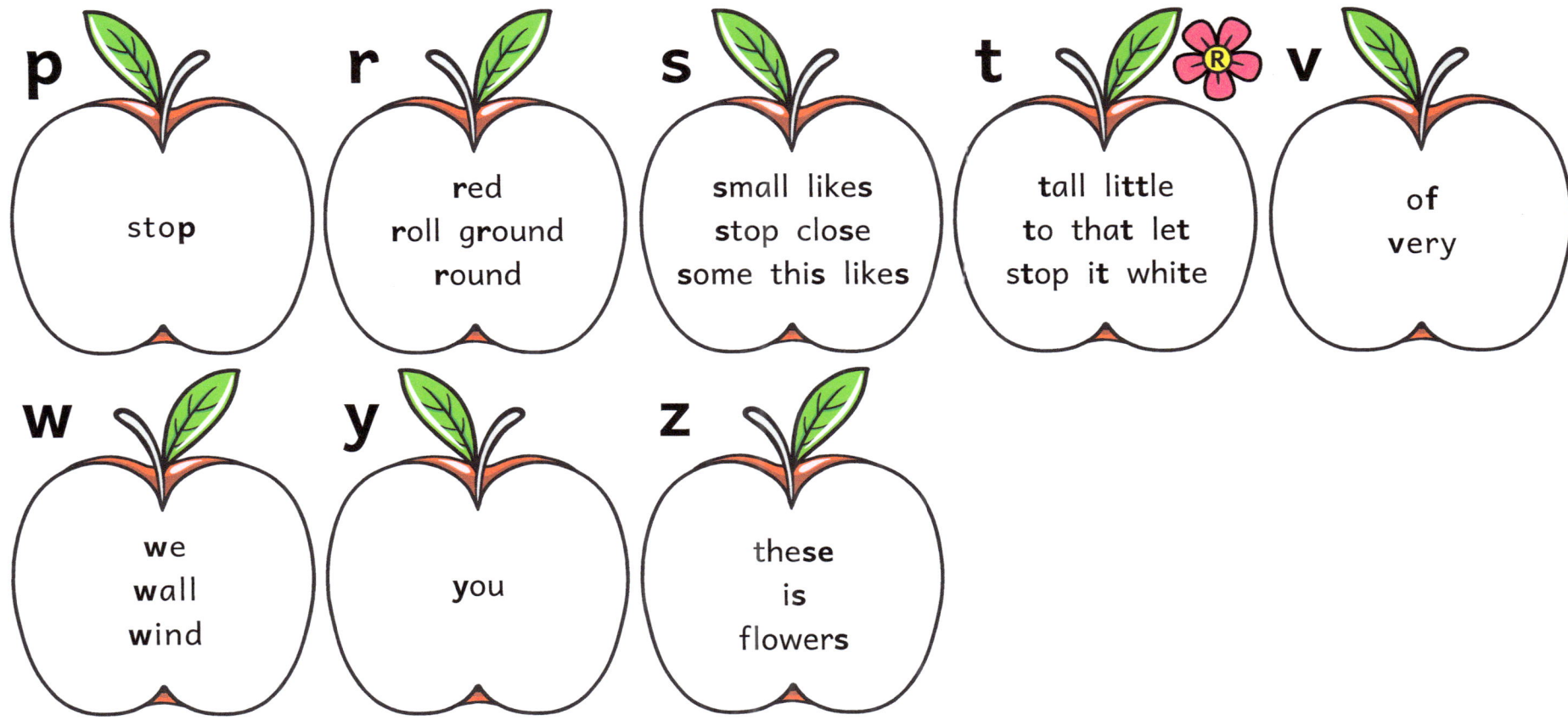

I Like - Book 3

Apple Core words in the Core word reading book	Other words in the Core word reading book
I, like, the, it, he, she, more, they, we, you, this, that, and	mum, dad, bug, two, one, lizard, likes

Decodable text focus	Other words in the Decodable text
'ug' words: pug, rug, bug, hug, mug	a, sat, on, the, can, see, want/s, to, no, does, not, crept, under, that, into, near, said, yes

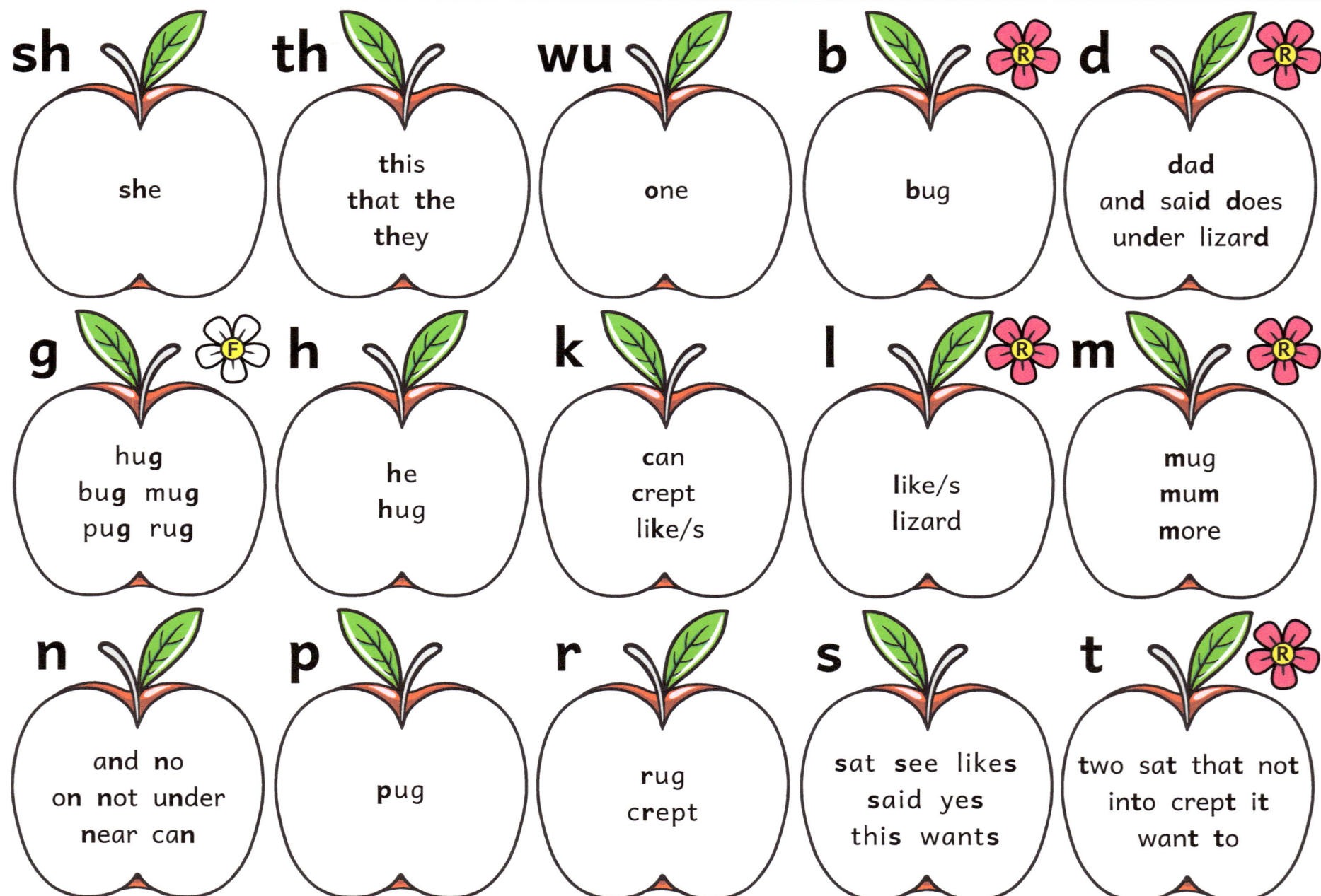

Series: 1 - I Like **Book: 3**

w — we, want/s

y — you, yes

z — does, lizard

I Like - Book 4

Apple Core words in the Core word reading book	Other words in the Core word reading book
I, like, the, it, he, she, more, they, we, you, this, that, and, to, look, up, down, there, here	mum, dad, at, frog, bug, likes

Decodable text focus	Other words in the Decodable text
'op' words: hop, mop, top, stop, pop	look, at, the, frog, up, there, on, of, that, are, bubbles, them, go, just, like, you, and, down, they, floor

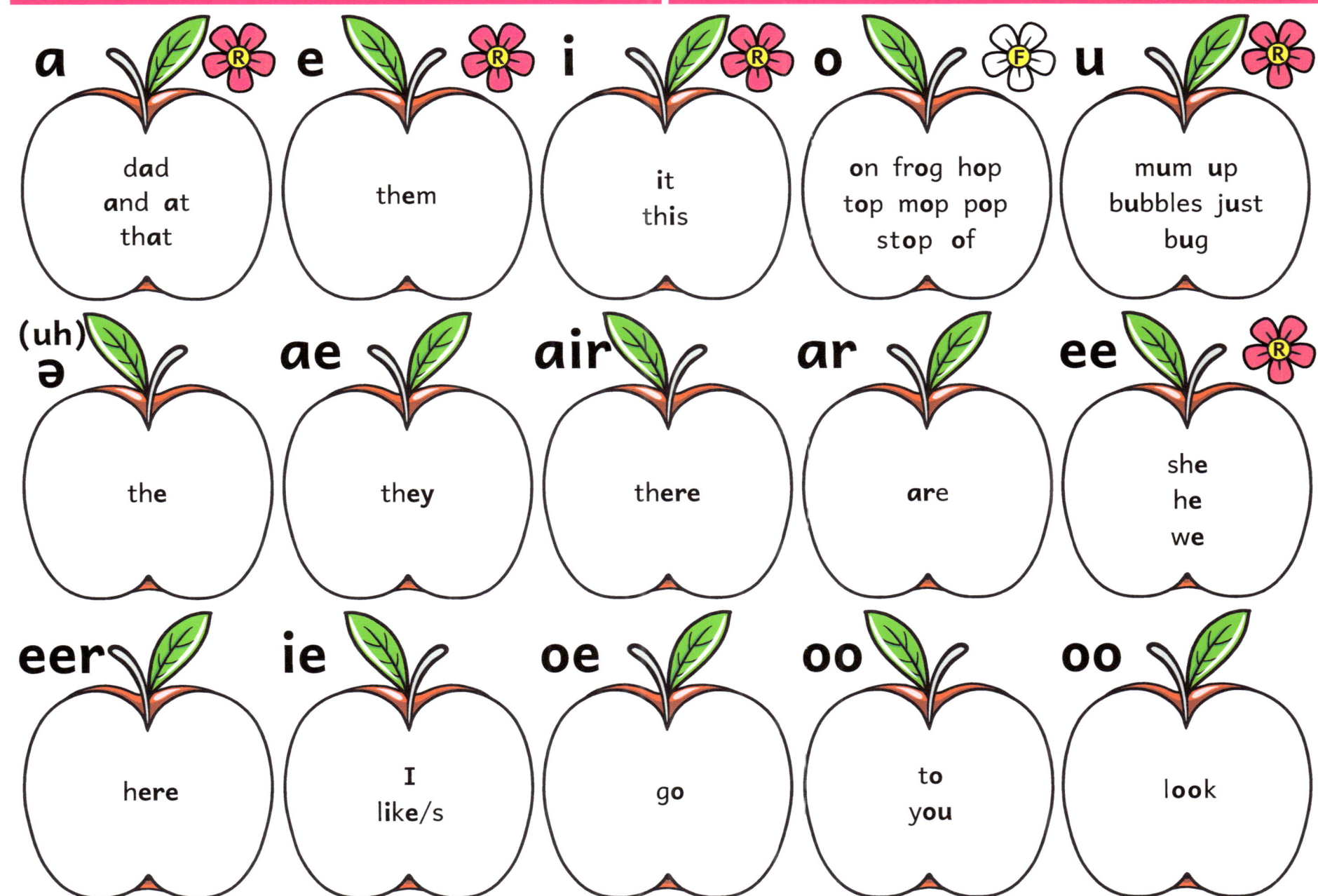

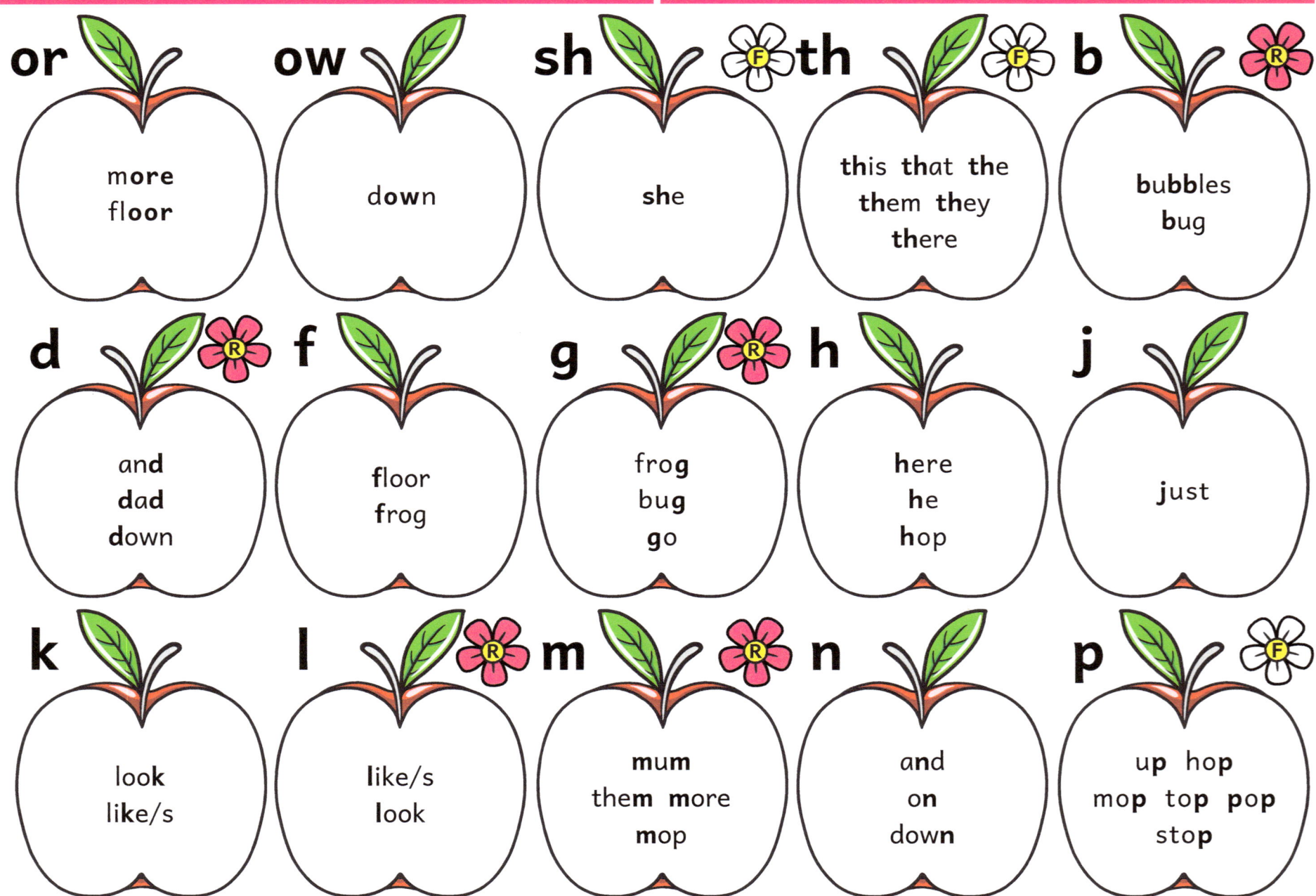

Series: 1 - I Like | **Book: 4**

- **r**: frog
- **s**: this, stop, likes
- **t**: just, at, to, that, top, stop, it
- **v**: of
- **w**: we
- **y**: you
- **z**: bubbles

I Like - Book 5

Apple Core words in the Core word reading book	Other words in the Core word reading book
I, like, the, it, he, she, more, they, we, you, this, that, and, to, look, up, down, there, here, not, do	mum, dad, at, too, spider, likes

Decodable text focus	Other words in the Decodable text
'at' words: fat, bat, sat, mat, cat, rat, that	the, on, a, with, can, see, that, and, is, I, like, you, we, do, they

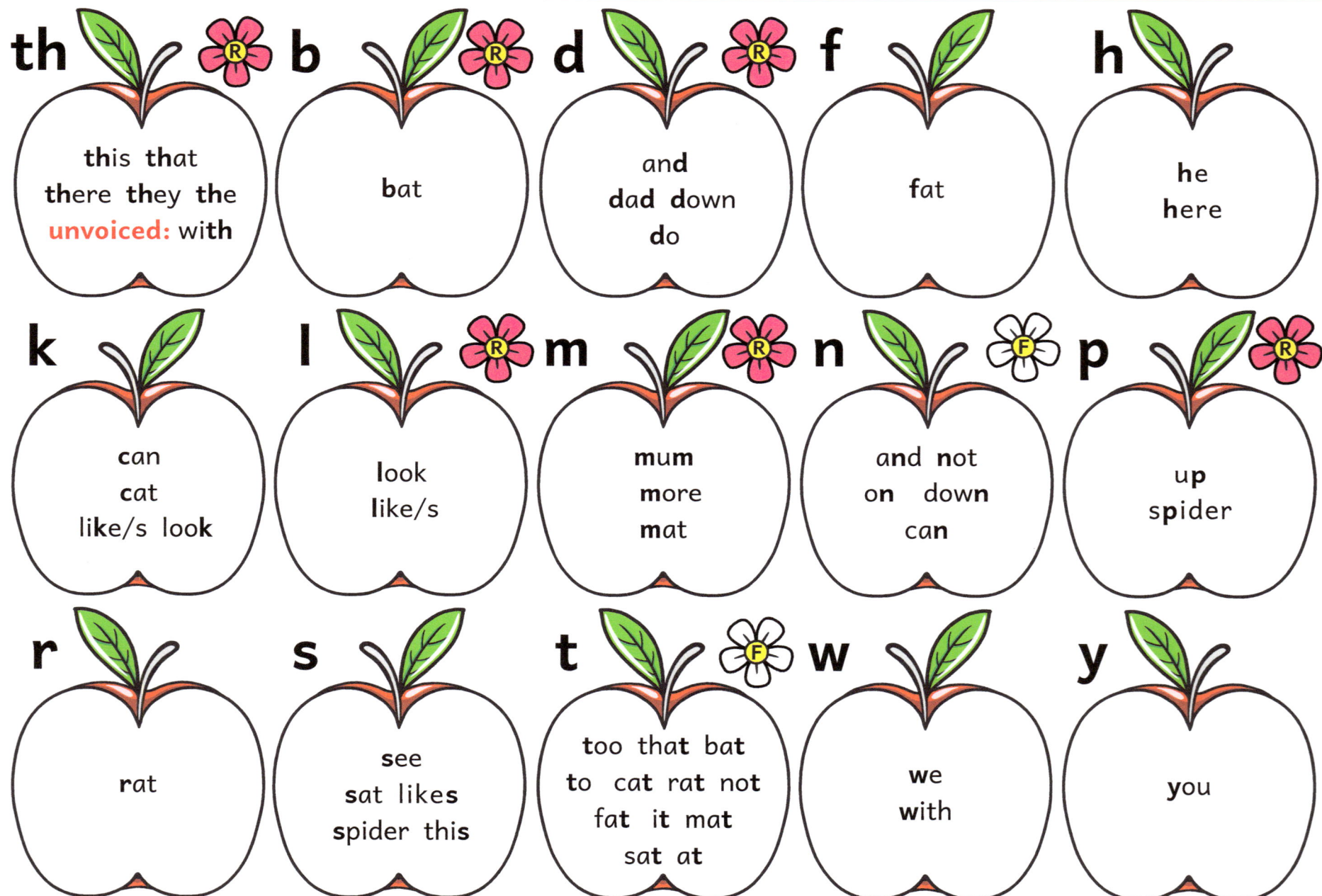

Series: 1 - I Like **Book: 5**

VZee

VeeZee Publications

Wait, there's more!

Visit our website for information about our range of readers & supporting products.

veezeepublications.com

www.ingramcontent.com/pod-product-compliance
Lightning Source LLC
Chambersburg PA
CBHW042106090526
44590CB00004B/118